BLUE HEART AFTERNOON

Nigel Gearing

BLUE HEART AFTERNOON

A Comedy of Betrayal

OBERON BOOKS
LONDON

WWW.OBERONBOOKS.COM

First published in 2012 by Oberon Books Ltd
521 Caledonian Road, London N7 9RH
Tel: +44 (0) 20 7607 3637 / Fax: +44 (0) 20 7607 3629
e-mail: info@oberonbooks.com
www.oberonbooks.com
Reprinted in 2012

A catalogue record for this book is available from the British Library.

PB ISBN: 978-1-84943-139-2
Digital ISBN: 978-1-84943-266-5

Cover image by istock

Printed, bound and converted
by CPI Group (UK) Ltd, Croydon, CR0 4YY.

Visit www.oberonbooks.com to read more about all our books
and to buy them. You will also find features, author interviews and
news of any author events, and you can sign up for e-newsletters
so that you're always first to hear about our new releases.

For Greg and Pascale

Blue Heart Afternoon was first performed at Hampstead Theatre Downstairs on April 5, 2012 with the following cast:

DIVA	Sian Thomas
SONGWRITER	Steve Noonan
INGENUE	Ruby Bentall
'JANITOR'	Peter Marinker

Director	Tamara Harvey
Designer	Lucy Osborne
Composer	Michael Bruce
Sound Designer	Emma Laxton
Lighting Designer	Johanna Town
Casting	Sam Chandley
Production Manager	Bob Holmes

This is the text of the play in the first week of rehearsal.

N.G.

'If Gershwin's songs are representative of the '20s (…) Arlen's songs carry in them the haunting melancholy of a sadder, perhaps even wiser time.'

Edward Jablonksi:
'Harold Arlen – Happy With the Blues'

* * *

'Below-the-title billing was a low to which she [Dietrich] had not sunk since <u>The Blue Angel</u>. Her <u>Kismet</u> function was to decorate the harem (though the Code would not let them call it that), warble a few 'Oriental' tunes by Harold Arlen and E.Y. Harburg (woefully far from <u>Oz</u>) and provide legs.'

Steven Bach: 'Marlene'

* * *

'He [Elia Kazan] had always said he came from survivors and that the job was to survive… Had I been of his generation, he would have had to sacrifice me as well.'

Arthur Miller (writing of the HUAC proceedings):
'Timebends'

* * *

Author's note:

Though inspired by the friendship between Harold Arlen and Marlene Dietrich, this play is a fiction with fictional characters.

Characters

Los Angeles, 1951.

In the darkness the sound of distant surf and wind-blown palm trees.

Static from a radio modulates into a few bars from 'Blues In The Night' and back into static before cutting out abruptly.

Backlit against a doorway, an elderly man in coat and hat carrying a suitcase.

'JANITOR': Consider this… A man goes away from his home, lies in strange beds in the dark. He crosses seas and continents, builds cabins and cities. Finally, on this last coast of all – here where the world ends amid temperate air, fragrant with orange-blossom – he builds houses big with gables he remembers from Vienna, shady Spanish courtyards like a dream of Old Seville, castles worthy of any Scottish laird.

And the <u>real</u> him? The culture he's carried with him on railways from station-locker to station-locker and hidden in empty hotel wardrobes and broken and patched together like a Ming vase? What d'you know. Here, of a sudden, it's irrelevant. It don't mean a thing. All he can do is throw it away and start over.

'America. Eat me up'…

Light dims to darkness.

Lights up on a woman (20-ish) at present wearing only underwear and heels. She puts on the monogrammed cap of a restaurant waitress, posing as if to someone offstage.

INGENUE: How d'you like me, Mr Case?

No response.

Mr Case? Are you all right in there?

Still no response. She frowns slightly, and begins to put on other pieces of clothing which have been scattered on the chesterfield behind her.

The room in which she is standing is the comfortable but unadorned living room of a ground-floor apartment on or near Pacific Palisades (the latter just visible perhaps through a window upstage right).

11

Polished wood floors; a white baby grand; a white bear-rug; a cocktail trolley and on it a telephone, pad and silver pen; a winged armchair and, beside it, a small side-table with carafe and ice-bucket and a gold (Oscar) statuette.

As she finishes dressing – she is wearing the colour-coded skirt, monogrammed blouse and cap of a restaurant waitress – SONGWRITER comes on. He is dressed in white flannels, a white short-sleeved shirt and a white sweater across his shoulders. In his hand he holds a tennis-racquet and as he talks practises the odd stroke.

INGENUE: Well, good morning!

SW: Good morning to you too, Jennifer!

INGENUE: Gee, you're all kitted out.

SW: Look who's talking. *(Smiles. Shrugs.)* 'The Country Club'. They expect no less. My <u>tennis-partner</u> expects no less.

INGENUE: Is that right?

SW: And a guy needs to look his best if he's hoping to *(Gestures with racquet.)* – pirouette – sashay – twin-step his way to victory!

INGENUE: This is tennis?

SW: I <u>am</u> playing with Fred Astaire…

INGENUE: Gee. So I guess you must know 'Miss Rogers' too?

SW: Uh-huh.

INGENUE: And Mr Gable?

SW: 'Clark Gable'?

She nods enthusiastically.

SW: Mm. Let me see. Ain't he the wine-waiter over at the Cocoanut Grove?

INGENUE: Hey. Now you're joshing me. I might be new to Hollywood, but I ain't <u>that</u> dumb!

SW: Now who'd ever imagine you were?

INGENUE: I'm from Texas, ain't I? I've heard the jokes.

SW: Tell me a joke about Texas, Jennifer. *(Another tennis-stroke.)* Something to put Mr Astaire off his stroke.

INGENUE: Ain't that a bit 'unethical'?

SW: You <u>are</u> new to Hollywood.

They both laugh amiably. But suddenly she registers the gold statuette behind the carafe.

INGENUE: Hey. That's your Oscar, right?

SW: Right.

She picks it up admiringly.

INGENUE: 'Academy Award . To "Blue Heart Afternoon". Original song. Music and lyrics by Ernest Case. 1950'

You must be so proud. I guess by now half the world must have heard that song.

But, still smiling, SONGWRITER has looked pointedly at his watch.

SW: Now if you're gonna make your shift…

INGENUE: Oh right. Listen, Mr Case –

SW: Please. 'Ernie'.

INGENUE: It's been real swell. 'Ernie'. What say we do this again –

SW: Sure.

INGENUE: – Catch a movie? Grab a bite?

SW: I'll call you.

INGENUE: You don't have my number.

SW: Ah.

INGENUE: …But maybe that's how you like it?

SW: Come now.

INGENUE: ...And, Mr Case, I don't want to seem pushy but... but you did talk about this new movie you're composing the music for? With maybe – just maybe – a part for me? For that you'll need my number, right?

SW: Right.

He takes the pen and notepad from next to the telephone, passes them to her. She begins to write her number, only to stop at the sight of a name already on the pad.

INGENUE: Gee. Mr Case. Ernie. You know Liese Felsing?

SW: Only by reputation.

INGENUE: You gonna work with her maybe?

SW: Maybe.

INGENUE: She's the biggest star in all of Hollywood!

SW: Still? Her last movie, they say those that stayed till the end shared the same cab home.

INGENUE: Did you never see that very first picture she made? The dark end of the street with just the light from the gas-station behind her. She turns back toward the camera, she throws that last goodbye kiss...and then she's gone with only the memory of her beret, that trench-coat, to tell you she was ever there at all. Now that was a great picture!

SW: Right...

INGENUE: Is it true what they say? They say Adolf Hitler or one of them guys went down on his knees and begged her to come back to Europe. But she said: 'Mr Hitler, I refuse to come back as long as you and your kind are in power. Mr Hitler, I will continue to refuse just as long as...'

Still smiling politely, he has looked pointedly at his watch. A beat as he waits for her to remember to write her name and number on the pad. Finally doing so:

Well, I think you're very lucky, Mr Case! I'd do anything to work with her... But, hey, I guess I'd better be going, right?

SW: Back to the Salad Bar?

INGENUE: And how! I got quite a day. Later I gotta work Cocktail Hour <u>and</u> First Dinner. But they were real nice: they said as long as I punch in early and lay them tables for First Luncheon then I could still make my meeting.

SW: [Your 'meeting']?

INGENUE: Right. *(Suddenly a little shy.)* This afternoon I got this audition. At the office of Mister Konig?

SW: 'Harry Konig, Head of Studio'? Be careful, Jennifer. The way I heard it, the last actress he 'auditioned' he chased round his desk for an hour or more. Of course, you may be all right...

INGENUE: ?

SW: He's so old that if he catches up with you he won't remember why he was chasing you in the first place.

INGENUE: Mr Case? Are you being entirely fair? My understanding was, he's a man of great culture.

SW: Oh yeh? Last thing <u>I</u> heard he was planning a movie about Adam and Eve. With a cast of thousands.

INGENUE: So – okay! – who's <u>your</u> producer at the moment?

He looks skyward and beats his chest with his fist.

SW: Can't you guess?

INGENUE: And you – so big 'n' famous 'n' all – you telling me you never needed a helping hand when you was still scrabbling for a break?

SW: Jennifer. I apologize.

He takes back the notebook from her, gives her a farewell peck on the cheek.

Send Harry my love. Tell him...tell him...'the project', I'm, er, on the case.

INGENUE goes. He looks a moment at the notepad, tears off the girl's sheet and folding it puts it in his backpocket. For a moment he contemplates the earlier sheet on the notepad. He walks over to the telephone, picks up the receiver, dials a single number.

SW: Hi, Mavis? Still no luck with that number? … Keep trying, will you?

The silhouette of DIVA appears in the doorway.

He looks up and puts the phone down. Light change.

SW: It was late last summer.

I'd dropped off Elizabeth, my wife, at her folks' back East and decided for the hell of it to drive back here to LA. Five days on my own, five days on the road to think through some tunes I had in my head but hadn't quite nailed… So I'm driving through Okie country – tumbleweeds, chicken-coops, dirt-poor rednecks and even poorer coloreds – and I stop for gas in some forgotten hick town where there'd been a county fair just the week before, and there – still – was the stage and a few high-school kids foolin' around on it where someone had rigged up a little spotlight and was running it off the juice of a truck parked right by.

It was dusk now. Desert-blue. And suddenly stepping into the light, with a beat-up electric guitar, was this kid, all of sixteen maybe, wearing denims and a grin as wide and bright as the stage. What was he playing on that piss-poor ten-dollar Fender of his? You tell me. It was both familiar and like nothin' I'd ever heard in my life. There was the beat, of course – my God, yes, <u>what</u> a beat! As for the rest: jump-blues, fast twelve-bars, some old Country licks, even a bit of Gospel… The kids around him were going wild.

Oh – and I forgot to mention. This boy. He was <u>white</u>.

Ever since, I been asking how long before even an Oscar loses its shine? How long before your name – my name, anyone's name – becomes a footnote if you're lucky, a punchline if you ain't…and then forgotten altogether? Ever

since, I been asking myself – this boy, this music, was it any
good?

It was more than good. It was The Future.

Lights dim to darkness, except for a spot of light caught by the cut-glass decanter and the tumbler next to it on a small side table. We are now in an undefined office sanctum: a telephone rings, unanswered, then stops.

INGENUE appears: she has made herself slightly more demure by means of a cloth-flower pinned to the front of her blouse.

The silence is followed by the faintest of coughs from elsewhere in the room.

INGENUE: Hello? Is somebody there?

Light expands to take in the winged armchair beside the side table, and the elderly man seen earlier now seated with his hands crossed on his lap. He is short, wears shiny shoes and a rather old-fashioned suit.

INGENUE: Excuse me. I thought… I guess I got the wrong
door, right?

'JANITOR': Young lady, if you're looking for who I think you
are you shoulda turned left at the water cooler.

INGENUE: I'm sorry. In that case I'll –

'JANITOR': No need. No need. *(He gestures into the darkness.)* But
just remember: 'Abandon hope all ye who enter here'.

INGENUE: Sir?

'JANITOR': 'Auditions', right? Or maybe you had some more
…'private business'? No matter! Same room! Same b –

…But the old man has started to cough. The coughing continues and turns very bad. He seems about to fall off his chair.

INGENUE: Say. Can I…

The old man gestures as best he can to the water carafe just out of reach while, still choking, he finds in his waistcoat pocket a small snuff-box. INGENUE anxiously pours him a glass of water; he passes her the snuff-box giving her to understand that he needs something from inside it. She taps out first one then two small pills, which he takes and swallows with more water.

Eventually something like normality resumes, the old man looking exhausted and INGENUE helpless. Finally:

'JANITOR': Thank you. Maybe you just gave an old man one more year of life. *(He's started to rally. Seeing her as if for the first time:)* Then again, maybe I died already and you the Angel of Mercy... Say, you got tits on you like a man rarely sees this side of Mortality. *(Smiles.)* Pardon my language, young lady. It is calculated to obscure my natural refinement and suggest a quintessential vulgarity.

INGENUE: Then I'd say it's doing a pretty good job.

He has reached across to hand her back the glass. As she takes it, and despite his frailty, he nimbly plucks INGENUE's rosette from her blouse-front.

INGENUE: Hey –

She puts down the glass, holds out her hand.

Can I have my flower back, please?

'JANITOR': *(Grasping her hand a moment.)* I'd say you were a size six, right?

INGENUE: Pardon me? *(She blushes, withdraws her hand quickly and covers her chest with it.)*

'JANITOR': *(Smiles again.)* I'm referring to the size of your hand, young lady – not your chest. A 'six', right?

Mystified, INGENUE nods warily.

Of course I'm right. Gloves. Ladies' gloves. It's where I made my first buck.

See, there was this ball-breaker of a tariff on all pairs of gloves imported into the US. Me, I'd order from back home a dozen crates of left-hand gloves only, to be delivered to, say, San Diego, and a dozen crates of right-hand gloves only, to be delivered to maybe Santa Barbara... And when no one showed up to claim them and they'd go for a knock-down auction as Uncollected Imports of little use to anyone – I mean, who wants only a left-hand glove or only a right-hand glove? – well, that's where I cleaned up. I'd get 'em for a song and jus' sling 'em together.

Yes. A size 'six'.

INGENUE: Excuse me. This is very interesting but…

'JANITOR': …But you'd like to see Head of Casting. Am I right?

Still wary, she nods.

Maybe – if you get real lucky – Head of Production? Maybe even…Head of Studio – 'Harry Konig' himself?

Again she nods warily.

So maybe I could make an introduction.

INGENUE: Who'd you say you were?

'JANITOR': Just call me the 'manager of the store'. I count 'em in and I count 'em out, remembering when possible to turn off the lights.

INGENUE: Oh I get it. The janitor… Thanks all the same. I can make my own introductions.

'JANITOR': I'm sure you can. *(He smiles.)* Just as long as someone shows you the right door. *(Smiles again.)* You know today I quit my job. Today I decided: let some other mother's child turn out the lights. Is this why all of a sudden I'm getting these memories? And you in there with them?

INGENUE: Pardon me?

'JANITOR': You remind me of someone. Half a lifetime ago. A salon in the afternoon. Late sunlight, deep carpets, girls in gowns whose price was not negotiable… And amid the music – operetta maybe, some dance music certainly – amid this music and the cigarette smoke and the calculated passions…

Already I was way too old for her. I who had never been to a house like this before – aged forty, had crossed and re-crossed the Atlantic, but had known until then only one woman, my wife – I said, 'Liebchen. Come with me and I shall make you a star'. And I did just that...

It coulda been yesterday. It coulda been you.

INGENUE looks quickly at her wristwatch.

INGENUE: Sir, I got this appointment –

He smiles.

'JANITOR': I heard a joke today. 'Who'd want to live till they're ninety-seven?'

INGENUE: 'Someone who's ninety-six'?

'JANITOR': You're smart.

INGENUE: I just serve a lot of tables. I get to hear all the gags. All the <u>old</u> gags.

'JANITOR': Here's another. There's this real old guy who has to decide between dying peaceful, with dignity, his family all around him...or screwing this beautiful young girl and most likely going out flagrante – a cardiac with all flags flying. What would you say?

INGENUE: I'd say that depended on the girl.

'JANITOR': Yeh? So is the girl saying 'yes'?

INGENUE blinks: she is saying nothing. A moment. He tugs at his ear.

Gee. That's the worst thing about getting old. You start to go deaf?

INGENUE smiles slightly despite herself.

What d'you say I take some new measurements? This time your weight?

He starts to move in on her.

Yes?

Yes?

Yes?

...But the phone rings.

Goddam...

'JANITOR' picks up phone.

(Harsh.) Yes? *(Exploding.)* How many more times? I'm taking no more meetings! I'm seeing no one! Niemand. Personne. And if I could, I'd say it in Polack too!

He slams down the phone. Turning, he seems old again. He smiles wearily.

Excuse me.

INGENUE: That was your wife?

'JANITOR': No. With my wife I get <u>aggressive</u>.

INGENUE: Tell me something. Since when does a 'janitor' take 'meetings'?

'JANITOR': I <u>said</u> you were smart...

INGENUE: And 'the girl'?

'JANITOR': Excuse me?

INGENUE: 'The girl in the salon'? What became of her?

Pause.

'JANITOR': Her memory alone continues to spill down light on me. To open my days like a flower and in the evening to chase the stars round the sky like the stoplights on Mulholland...

For a moment, still smiling, he is lost to the memory. Finally he comes out of it...

'What became of her?'

'JANITOR' gives another rueful smile and a gentle shake of the head:

Don't even ask.

Pause. He realizes he is still holding the cloth-rosette.

Your flower…

A little unsteadily he moves towards her, gives her the flower, gesturing as he does so to the door.

Why not take <u>that</u> door. 'The Casting Suite'. A shortcut to your future? Oh yes… And be sure to say 'goodbye' with a smile: you may want to come back.

She smiles, nods.

INGENUE: Goodbye.

He turns away. With the slightest of bemused shrugs she turns to leave.

Light change.

Lights up on SONGWRITER, as before. Standing watching him in the doorway is DIVA, wearing a blouse, a light blouson and slacks with sunglasses in her hair.

DIVA: Excuse me. Would you be 'Mr – *(She fusses a moment, trying to focus on a notepad slip of her own.)*

SW: *(Not unkindly.)* You see anyone else here, Ma'am?

DIVA: There <u>was</u> this cleavage in a uniform. As I came in.

SW: 'Cleavage'?

DIVA: Sure. Redhead, wide lapels. I could feel her tits pushing up against me from the other side of the lobby.

SW: And that's a big lobby.

DIVA: Try not to brag, Mr –

SW: Case. Ernie Case.

DIVA: – Mr Case… I suspect the lobby, like the cleavage, is yours for the renting only. Am I right?

SW: Short-term lease. Property of the studio. *(Smiles. Very Groucho Marx:)* But I won't hear a word against her.

DIVA: Should I disagree? A face unclouded by thought…and some of the finest epidermis I ever saw in my life.

SW: Another kid who wants to act.

DIVA: You don't say.

He ushers her in.

SW: So welcome. And thank you for coming. I've been trying to reach you for three days.

DIVA: Three days only?

SW: It's about the project.

DIVA: Uh-huh.

SW: The Harry Konig project.

DIVA: You know Harry?

SW: Sure. And he knows you. 'S why you're here, right?

DIVA: I'm here 'cos I want to be. You like him?

SW: Harry? He's a producer. To know him is to like him. Not to know him is to love him.

DIVA: And the project?

SW: You read the script?

DIVA: Has Harry, I wonder?

SW: Harry don't read too much. His lips get tired after ten pages… But he has a nose for these things. Like something in there got to him. And where Harry's nose leads, the rest of him follows. What d'you say? Something there? Something for you and me both?

DIVA: Why me? There are plenty of other actresses out there, Mr Case.

SW: …And all of them like the second pressing of the grape. *(Pause.)* Well?

DIVA: Sure I'm interested. Likewise my agent – who may be unbearable, may even be a crook – but not, I think, a fool. *(Nodding to the side table.)* That's your Oscar, right? Your star is rising, Mr Case, even while, elsewhere in the

23

firmament – *(She seems to leave the thought unfinished. Pause.)*
Tell me something. I believe you knew Buddie, right?

SW: Buddie Goldman? Sure.

DIVA: May he rest in peace.

SW: *(Nods. A difficult pause. Turning away again.)* Hey, what say
I get you a drink and tell you my idea? A coffee maybe?
Maybe something stronger?

She looks at her expensive wristwatch.

DIVA: Give me five minutes and make it a Double Bourbon,
will you? I'm not an alcoholic, Mr Case –

SW: Call me 'Ernie'.

DIVA: – Just nostalgic for civilization.

*He gestures for her to sit down on the chesterfield. She does so, wearily
stretching out her legs. (She is surely aware these are a major asset).
He leans against one end of the divan, studying her with amusement,
waiting for more.*

DIVA: I went to the Desert. You should try it, Mr Case…
Fifteen minutes' drive from LA and then for a hundred
miles you'll see maybe one store, one service station. Up
through the San Gabriel mountains, the Western edge
of the Mojave. On to Death Valley and the LA Viaduct.
There the nights are so cool, the air so dry and blue. And
– above all – so empty of sound. And of movement… And
of men.

Pause.

This is America, no? To leave behind all you've created?
To start brand new and keep going, always further West?

SW: Further West than LA?

DIVA: *(Shrugs.)* The New Territory. It is only occasionally
'geographical'…Mind if I smoke?

He nods amiably and reaches for a glass ashtray on the cocktail trolley. She has taken a cigarette from a pack in her blouson pocket. He gives her a light from a heavy table lighter also on the cocktail trolley.

SW: And when you got to your desert, what did you do there?

DIVA: I pretended – without success – that I did not want a Double Bourbon on the rocks. I told myself I did not want to go back to a shower and ventilators and *(Does she look round?)* ...sour rooms webbed in dust.

SW: *(Smiles. Apologetic.)* It's the sand. It gets through all the cracks.

DIVA: You don't say.

SW: One day they reckon we won't need to go to the desert. It will come to us – reclaiming its own. The whole of Southern California. Meanwhile we have a maid who... *(Shrugs. Smiles boyishly.)* Hey. The shower is terrific. Wanna shake some dust from those clothes of yours and freshen up?

DIVA: You said 'we'?

SW: Me and my, er, wife.

DIVA: And where, Mr Case, is your 'er-wife'?

SW: Back East. Her nephew's First Holy Communion.

DIVA: But you are a Jew, no?

SW: Not my wife.

She looks at him a moment, then runs the index finger of her free hand along the base of the chesterfield, inspects it.

DIVA: I think this maid she is not so bad after all.

SW: How about I fix you that Bourbon?

She smiles, nods. As he busies himself at the trolley:

DIVA: So. This movie of yours? You gonna give me the Official Tour?

SW: Okay. Establishing shot: an overhead of New York, early evening. Snow's falling. Standing at a window is a dame as mature as she is beautiful – but also with just a hint of sadness. Call her Anna... Okay so far?

DIVA: Uh-huh.

SW: A close-up of the dame dissolves into the same face a few years earlier. It's France under the Occupation and Anna, a cabaret legend, is seen singing in a ritzy Parisian night club – a club, as it happens, frequented by Nazi officers. If Anna seems nice towards these officers in a way some of her old pals, now in the Resistance, resent and criticize her for, well, she has her reasons.

We'll come to that... Her young dresser Fleur has no such reasons. She flirts 'cos she flirts, a good-time girl. Still clear?

DIVA: As crystal.

SW: Turns out that Anna's husband Stephan – a famously gifted composer, but also famously anti-Fascist and a Jew – has not just 'disappeared' as Anna has led everyone to believe, but is in fact holed up in the club's basement where – even now, when he's hiding from the Gestapo – he is desperately trying to finish his magnum opus, his Symphony for Peace –

DIVA: No prizes for guessing who's doing the music for this movie, right?

SW: – a Symphony blending Old World Jewish folk-songs, gypsy dances, New World strains of Negro spirituals, Dixieland... But now, it transpires, an indiscretion from Fleur has alerted the Nazis to Stephan's presence. All three of them – Anna, Stephan and Fleur – make a late-night dash for the coast and the first available boat out of Le Havre...

DIVA: Mister, haven't I heard this somewhere before? Is this some kind of 're-make'?

SW: Wait –

DIVA: Not that I've got anything against re-makes –

SW: <u>Wait</u>, I say –

DIVA: Sometimes I think they should do the 're-make' before they do the 'make'!

SW: Cut to French port. Night and fog. By the quayside is the fishing trawler that will take them to safety. The captain, an old soak, is crustily benign but even he's kinda jittery… Suddenly all the harbor arc-lights flash on! The Nazis have caught up with them. In her trademark trenchcoat and beret – conspicuous in the moonlight – Anna leads the Gestapo on a wild goose chase around the docks. Only to turn at the last moment, now when cornered, and reveal herself as… Fleur!

DIVA: *(Deadpan)* Well, Heavens above…

SW: Fleur, who has made the ultimate sacrifice for Anna and for her country, is shot dead and Stephan is fatally wounded. Just managing to drag him on board, Anna nurses his head in her lap as the boat sets sail. With his dying breath he entrusts to her the blood-soaked score of his just-completed symphony, whose opening strains we hear as now we dissolve back to New York City a couple of years later… A quick exterior shows us Anna is in a concert-hall whose posters proudly announce this, the première of Stephan's Symphony for Peace. She enters the packed auditorium. Before she can take her seat she receives a standing ovation from the men and women already there in evening dress, some of them those same Parisian friends who back in France had doubted her commitment to Freedom and Justice. As the orchestra plays on, slow fade to black. End of movie.

Pause.

DIVA: And me? I get to play the fishing-boat 'captain'? The 'old soak'? 'Crustily benign?'

SW: What d'you say, Diva? I may call you 'Diva'?

DIVA merely raises an eyebrow, neither accepting nor protesting.

DIVA: Europe and America?

SW: Right!

DIVA: Tragedy and reconciliation?

SW: Right! And along with it a whole tapestry of sound, more than just another 'tra-la-la'. A Symphony For Our Time? A Meditation on Old Worlds and New?

DIVA: No kidding.

SW: You know all this. Who better? You saw the horror and protested and came away… And then rode into Berlin shoulder to shoulder with General Patton on his tank, saw Belsen two days after it was opened up. *(Smiles.)* Of course, others would say – my grandfather among them – 'So being defeated wasn't enough for you?'

DIVA: I wasn't defeated. I was victorious.

SW: A figure of speech… We know what we're talking about, you and I. Your eyes. They're like my grandfather's: they have an old and European pity. *(Beat.)* … And maybe just once in our lives we get to work on something with meaning, something with depth. This time round we do a project – you and I – we can be proud of !

DIVA: Er… 'this time round'?

SW: I –

DIVA: Do I take it you saw my last movie?

SW: Sure. I, er – I can't begin to tell you how much I admired it –

DIVA: Try.

SONGWRITER laughs, throws up his hands.

SW: So that movie stank. So what? This time – believe me – it'll be different !

Pause as SONGWRITER 'rests his case'. If not before, he now hands her her drink.

DIVA: Am I missing something here, Big Boy? In this movie – in your movie – 'Anna' doesn't associate with the Resistance because that way she can better protect 'Stephan'?

SW: Correct.

DIVA: So if she seems too chummy with the Nazis –

SW: She's playing by her own rules.

DIVA: Not like Fleur –

SW: Who is too chummy, but will eventually redeem herself by the ultimate sacrifice.

Pause.

DIVA: So let me get this clear. Anna fraternizes with the Nazis 'cos she's looking out for her own…

SW: Well…

DIVA: And, of course, her husband's priceless music.

SW: *(Nods.)* His symphony.

DIVA: I mean to say – what's more important than this man's music, right?

SW: Right! *(Beat, sensing irony.)* You got a problem with that?

DIVA: So who are you in this?

SW: [Me]?

DIVA: The haunted Jewish composer, whose genius is only recognised after his death?

SW: Hey –

DIVA: Or 'Fleur', who maybe betrayed her friends but is ready to pay the ultimate price? Or – better still – 'Anna', who apparently snubs her old anti-Fascist pals 'cos she's playing a long game, 'cos she's understood some things are important beyond all this fiddle?

SW: Listen here –

DIVA: I mean to say, if Ernie – excuse me, 'Anna' – is prepared to sacrifice some old friends, if one or other of these goes down under enemy fire even – I mean what's this weighed against the <u>Art</u>, the <u>Music</u>?… *(Rising.)* Mind if I get myself some ice? Always I get my own ice.

SONGWRITER nods curtly. She rises, busies herself at the ice-bucket, breaking off some ice, adding it to her drink. Eventually turning:

Tell me something. You say you knew Buddie, right? You were a friend, I think?

SW: Uh-huh.

Pause. Holding her glass, she perhaps leans against the wall, scrutinising him.

DIVA: So tonight you come to the Event? At the Grill?

SW: Perhaps.

DIVA: I'm sorry?

Pause.

SW: These last months – Buddie, the whole gang, Larrie, Marvin and me. We'd drifted apart.

DIVA: And why was that, I wonder?

SW: I think you <u>know</u> why.

DIVA: 'Cos maybe their star was fading?

SW: 'Cos of that scumbag McCarthy! 'Cos one twitch left of center and you're a paid-up member of the Communist Party. 'Cos lately to be seen with those guys was professional suicide! *(Embarrassed, perhaps, at the choice of words.)* That is…

DIVA: And now Buddie has chosen a less 'professional', more 'personal' suicide?

Silence from SONGWRITER.

Pause. As she sits down again on the divan:

DIVA: That name of yours. 'Case'. What was it before?

SW: 'Kasicki' *(Pronunciation: Cashitski)* So what?

DIVA: And you are a devout Jew, Mr Case?

SW: You kidding? See that dimmer up there? *(He gestures.)* On Hanukkah it turns down a menorah.

DIVA: Even so – I think – of your people, their achievements, you are proud, no?

SW: So?

DIVA: So? Why change your name?

SW: Are you serious? '<u>Kasitski</u>'?

DIVA: So you could prove yourself a good American perhaps?

SW: Hey – that was years ago…

DIVA: But how very convenient <u>now</u>! Now – when you can dump your friends?

SW: Did I say that?

DIVA: This 'gang' of yours – most of them Jews, many of them Communists – were they not good Americans too?

SW: I'm not McCarthy –

DIVA: And here we have it, I think. You've come a long way from Europe. From the long, sad history of the Jew. But now I wonder if in your eyes you have come far enough. Always you are saying 'How close it all is. How recent.' Too close, too recent.

SW: I miss Bud. I had respect for Bud.

DIVA: He had respect for himself. I think Buddie's suicide was his way of saying to Harry Konig, 'You can't fire me. I quit.'

SW: I think Buddie's suicide was his way of saying to <u>God</u>, 'You can't fire me. I quit.'

DIVA: *(Smiles.)* Any difference these days?

SW: Sure. Sometimes God gets delusions of grandeur: thinks he's Harry Konig.

She smiles, despite herself, but does not let up.

DIVA: So what then is left of the Ernie Case who – they tell me – used to raise funds to fight against Fascism in Europe?

SW: Listen –

DIVA: What has become of him, I wonder? Who is he now?

SW: <u>Listen to me!</u>

He hesitates a moment, nods, moves over to the piano. He sits down. A pause. This is his party-piece: as he talks he will slowly begin to embellish his remarks with the odd atmospheric chord.

SW: I was raised in New York, right? Lower East Side. Five-, six-storey tenement buildings where the front stoop is always cracked and, well, you've seen 'em – inside the banisters are wobbly and the stairways ain't making no promises either… And here we lived: our family and hundreds of others just like us. And every parent or grandparent was – it seemed – an immigrant. And, of course, a Jew.

Come the summer, it'd get so hot first the kids then practically whole families would sleep out on the fire escape or the roof, like it was one huge dormitory. Only this old guy that lived under us – 'Mr Kosilowski' – would not sleep out. Rarely left the building at all. Spoke maybe fifty words of American and spent his entire days and evenings trying to get Europe on some home-made radio he'd cooked up.

So, one long summer evening this baby three floors above us starts screaming. From seven o'clock on, for hour after goddam hour. 'Meningitis', perhaps – who knows? But the mother can't be persuaded to either take him away or let go of him… First of all people try to 'understand'. A few of the younger ones start playing basketball down in the yard just to ignore it. Then the complaints begin. Some begin to get nasty, threaten to kill the baby <u>and</u> the mother both. But pretty soon everyone without exception is going kinda nuts…

And then, all of a sudden, crackling with static, going in and out of tune, is the sweetest music you ever heard.

He starts to play an appropriate music – austere but poignant. As he does so:

Mama said it was a tune 'from the Old Country'. Bullshit. It was no such thing – it was a song-cycle by Schubert – this I learned later – and it was old Kosilowski playing it on his radio, the volume turned way up high… And now – the damnedest thing – suddenly that baby isn't screaming any more and 'cos the <u>baby</u>'s gone quiet after all this time so has everyone else – stopped talking, arguing, laughing, cursing. Even the kids down in the yard have just gathered up their ball and gone inside without a murmur… And still the Schubert goes on and before you know it somehow the whole block has gone to sleep for the night like they've taken a drug or heard the greatest lullaby in the world.

Later I heard all manner of things – that the kid had died that night, that on the contrary the kid recovered and grew up to be a genius… To me it didn't matter. All I knew at that moment was the peace, the silence, the <u>awe</u> that fell on those people like showers of rain. I have only one word for it: 'religious'.

Slowly the music has undergone a transformation. Recognisably still the same piece and losing none of its poignancy, it has become a slow contemporary blues.

Who is Ernie Case? I'll tell ya. He is the man who has decided that when it comes to Solidarity, when it comes to Politics, well, he ain't so good. What is he good at? Writing music. Of the kind that will stop 'em in their tracks and make 'em think again. Silence them with Beauty and turn 'em around. Like this movie.

Pause. He stops playing.

DIVA: Something tells me that Buddie – the late Buddie – will derive great consolation from that.

SW: *(Exasperated)* Diva! –

DIVA: And what about them others?

SW: ?

DIVA: Them others you mentioned. 'Marvin', 'Larrie' and the rest?

SW: They had it coming.

DIVA: Pardon me?

SW: Buddie was just a dreamer, a poor sap, an amiable over-educated drunk. But the rest? The other writers, the actors, the ego-crazed directors? I'll tell you. 'The fight against Fascism'? – that's one thing. But <u>their</u> tragedy? It was the day someone convinced 'em that after all the years of whoring and of pimping their small talent at a <u>very</u> high price to the 'degrading', 'demeaning' movies...they could redeem themselves and be <u>reborn</u> in the name of Uncle Jo Stalin and the Working Man! Never mind what 'Uncle Jo' <u>did</u> to the Working Man, what he did to the kulaks and the Jews back in Europe... And now? Now they're out on a limb while in Washington that low-life McCarthy picks 'em off one by one.

I got no sympathy.

I got no sympathy because – guys like them? the fashion-followers? the bandwagon Bolsheviks? – I could have told 'em: you exercise your skills, you ring the bell the best you know how... And if that still don't light a fire against the darkness for you, if you still can't manage <u>that</u> – well – it's simple. You settle for another kind of music altogether. Not the Internationale. Not even – so help me – the Stars 'n' Stripes. No, you settle for the kind of music you hear ten blocks away at five o'clock every Friday afternoon: the sound of the boy on the studio motorbike bringing you your weekly paycheck.

Pause.

Let's cut to the chase. ...Diva – am I playing solo here? What say you and I we make beautiful music together?

DIVA: Would that be a Bechstein or a penny-whistle?

SW: And there's always the chick...

DIVA: Pardon me?

SW: In the movie? 'Fleur'? Who's so very young and so very beautiful? You met her already. 'Jennifer'. The broad in the lobby. She wants to act, so let her.

DIVA: What's she to me, Mister?

SW: Come now...

DIVA: Why should I care?

SW: 'S not what they say in the studio.

DIVA: What do they say in the studio, Mr Case?

SW: They say, 'How do we know Diva's got this thing about cleanliness...?'

DIVA: ?

SW: 'She has a woman in twice a week who "does" for her.' *(Pause. Ironic.)* Me, I say: hey – she just ain't met the right kind of boy yet.

DIVA: My my. How tongues do wag.

SW: Well? Is it true or not?

DIVA: Let's just say between you and Miss Cleavage...

SW: Yes?

DIVA: And now, slow as I am, I think at last I begin to understand. Where once upon a time there was a little

Jew-boy wanting to succeed in the big bad world of the American goy, and ashamed of being a Jew –

SW: 'Ashamed'?

DIVA: He changes his name, he marries a shiksa... Now, however, as he gets older and more successful... What's that latest song of yours? 'Purple Afternoon'? –

SW: '<u>Blue Heart</u> Afternoon'!

DIVA: – Yes indeed, while <u>that</u>'s still riding high, so it seems is he. And yet. And yet. He who as a boy used to hate the synagogue and all it stood for, now he spends long hours talking to his...father? His grandfather? Some kind of rabbi, maybe?

Now, above all, this boy become a man wants to tell the world – he wants to tell <u>me</u>! – that anyone who saw what happened to the Jews of Europe has a special place in his heart. He wants to tell the world that although he might have heaved his friends over the side of the sled, left them back there for the jackals of Washington –

SW: Hey –

DIVA: At least he still <u>cares</u>!

And me? The pure 'Aryan', beloved of Goebbels and the Nazis? Me who turned her back on it all? What then should be <u>my</u> reward?

It is for me and him, The Songwriter, each of us admiring the other's 'sensitivity' and 'sense of history', to make this his Reach For Glory together... And then – when it's over? –

SW: Well?

DIVA: To fuck each other stupid maybe?

SW: Why not?

DIVA: And the six million dead Jews? And the chimneys still smoking in Belsen two days after the Armistice?

Yes – I was there, little man, just as I was riding a tank with Our Boys, standing 'shoulder to shoulder', as you put it, with General Patton… But this is not for the tittle-tattle of you and me on a dull afternoon in Los Angeles. It is beyond 'conversation'.

And I say to you – whenever with your little story of suffering Jews, of overheated tenements and Music Conquering All, when, in this way, you think you are giving belated proof of your finer feelings, be very careful for every time you do this you are betraying the real suffering. You are misusing History. You are betraying Belsen and those six million dead Jews just as you betray those awesome, mysterious words – 'love', 'beauty', 'pain', 'sorrow' – you like so much in your little songs. You are using them only to bring forth a tear. To get the rest of us in the right sentimental mood while you serve your own purposes.

Pause. She turns away.

SW: *(Ironic.)* Er… Can we take it that's a 'no'? *(Beat.)*

Listen –

… But the phone rings. SONGWRITER moves to answer it.

SW: Yes?… What?… Sure. Tell him I'm on my way. Tell him – *(He looks obliquely at DIVA, turns away again almost immediately.)* Yes…some kind of 'interest'… Oh – and Mavis? – cancel my tennis with Astaire, will you? Tell him…tell him <u>anything</u>.

He puts down the phone, rather pleased with himself.

DIVA: Something wrong?

SW: On the contrary. Where were we?

DIVA: You were pitching and I was listening.

SW: Right.

DIVA: Penny-whistle or concert grand.

SW: Right. And that was a call from Harry Konig's office, saying get over there right away! I can tell him you're in, Diva? What d'you say? A 'definite maybe' at least?

DIVA: I –

Suddenly INGENUE walks back in.

INGENUE: Mr Case?

SW: Jennifer?

INGENUE: Me so anxious to make my meeting 'n' all, I guess I forgot my make-up box. *(Apologetically to DIVA.)* Begging your pardon for the interruption, Ma'am. *(Registering.)* Hey –

SW: I gotta go… Jennifer? See you out? Diva?

DIVA: *(Scrutinising JENNIFER. A beat.)* Maybe I'll stick around after all… Take that shower.

SW: Why not? Jennifer – Liese Felsing, Liese – Jennifer… Have yourself another drink. Both of you. After all…what's the rush?

He smiles at JENNIFER and at DIVA, who smile back.

He exits in high spirits, leaving DIVA and INGENUE looking at each other.

Gee. I… You're… Ain't you?

DIVA: What if I am?

INGENUE: I don't know, I… All my life, I… And now… Well.

DIVA: Tell me. Do you ever finish your sentences?

INGENUE: Sure. I… Sometimes. But…

DIVA holds it a moment, wryly scrutinizing INGENUE.

DIVA: You want to be an actress, right?

INGENUE: How did you guess?

DIVA: Then take my advice. Get yourself a script. <u>Any</u> script.

INGENUE: Right.

INGENUE has taken out a notebook and is scribbling something down.

DIVA: Do you write down every piece of advice you get round here?

INGENUE: Oh only if the advice is good. Like yours. And like Mr Case's. Mr Case has told me a whole lotta things.

DIVA: I bet.

INGENUE: First time we met he told me something he'd never revealed to another living soul. I was so moved. Seems like he grew up real poor in this tenement on the Lower East Side and one night there was this baby crying and –

DIVA: *(Cutting her off, dry.)* You don't say.

INGENUE: Ma'am? –

DIVA: Did he never tell you about your neck?

INGENUE: No. Why? Is there something I should –

DIVA: And that plunge between your boobs? … Yes, right there – where your sweat comes trickling down, pauses a moment, and glows like it's…deciding which way to go?

INGENUE: No. He never said any of that. He said… *(She stops, finally reading the situation.)* Oh.

DIVA: Never mind.

INGENUE: Miss – *(She can't bring herself to say the name.)* Mind if I ask you something? Like I been wanting to ask for years but, hey, I never thought I'd find myself, well, like this and…

DIVA: Go right ahead.

INGENUE: Those pants you're always wearing. Even in photos. Isn't that kinda…uncomfortable?

DIVA: On the contrary. You should try.

INGENUE: Oh I could never do that.

DIVA: Why not? You might get to like it. Maybe it'll give you more confidence. A sense of being in charge… But then maybe you don't want that.

INGENUE: Isn't being in charge a man's job? *(Shrugs.)* I guess I just want to look good.

DIVA: That also is easy.

INGENUE: It is?

DIVA: If you're a man you cock your head to one side slightly and smile with your mouth shut. If you're a woman – with legs like yours or mine – you kinda shift your weight from one leg to the other, tilting your hip as you do so. Like this –

She demonstrates. INGENUE laughs.

INGENUE: An' that's all?

DIVA: Oh no. That's only the day-to-day. You want I show you more?

INGENUE: Gee, I… Well, yes. Yes!

DIVA: Why don't you start by putting down that notebook?

As INGENUE does so, DIVA takes up position by a dimmer switch on the wall. She takes stock, moves over and reaches up with a pole-hook to poke a light, tilting its beam. She nods for INGENUE to move beneath it as she herself steps back.

During this:

DIVA: So how do you like LA?

INGENUE: I like it fine!

DIVA grimaces while she adjusts the dimmer switch.

Not you?

DIVA: Sure, I like LA. It's the only town in the world where you can wake up in the morning and listen to the birds coughing in the trees.

INGENUE looks bemused.

Hey – just a joke… You're right. Comedy is not my forte. Witness that last movie.

INGENUE: Gee, I thought your last movie was a whole lotta fun.

DIVA: You did? That's a pretty exclusive club you're in.

INGENUE: And my boyfriend – he laughed so much he nearly peed in my hand. *(Blushes. A quick hand to her mouth.)* Oops. Pardon me, Ma'am.

A moment as DIVA looks at her quizzically, smiling and cocking her head, pole-hook still held upright in her hand.

DIVA: Tell me. Are you as naive as you seem?

INGENUE: 'Naive' means dumb, right?

DIVA: Don't knock it, honey. It's every man's dream: a sexually-experienced virgin. What am I saying? The dream of some women too. *(She looks at her appraisingly a moment.)*

INGENUE: Maybe I should be getting along…

DIVA: Before we've had our 'lesson'? … See – back in Central Casting they'll tell you there's Country Cute and there's The Kind That Would Eat Their Young – and never the twain shall meet. Me, I say, 'Why limit your options?'

INGENUE blinks.

INGENUE: I guess you lost me again.

DIVA: I'll make it simple. Like to know how to be a star?

INGENUE: Well…yes. *(Laughs.)* Yes!

DIVA: 'Beauty is more than skin deep', right?

INGENUE: Right!

DIVA: Wrong. You wanna be remembered for your adorable pancreas? Okay. So here's what we do. Forget about The Integrity Of Your Soul, forget about The Real You – and concentrate on The Light.

INGENUE: Ma'am?

DIVA: You ready?

INGENUE nods. DIVA starts slowly to turn the dimmer switch.

DIVA: Look upward, baby. Find the light. Look at that light like you could no longer live without it.

Now straighten up. Tilt your head – and suddenly you've got cheekbones…

To the left. The right. A little more. Now your nose ain't so crooked…

Oh and you might at least <u>pretend</u> to be enjoying it… Not <u>too</u> much. The trick, sweetie, is to do nothing. But to do it <u>interesting</u>.

Once more. Up. Rock forward on your toes – you've lost the light… Up. Right. Left… Turn your shoulders a little.

Perfect.

INGENUE holds the pose for a moment – and indeed, for that moment, she is transformed.

DIVA brings the lights back to normal, starts to come downstage.

'The light on a woman's smile'. <u>This</u> is cinema and this is all you need.

INGENUE reaches for her notebook.

Don't write it down, liebchen. Just remember it. Remember it every time some jumped-up newsboy who calls himself a movie director says, 'Let's go for Natural Light.' Remember and tell him: 'Animals fuck in Natural Light. Flies squat on dog-poop in Natural Light.' You and me – we're different… You think you've got that?

INGENUE: I think I've got that, Miss – I mean, 'Liese', I mean –

DIVA: Why not just call me like everyone else does?

INGENUE: Right. I –

DIVA: Why not just call me… 'Diva'.

DIVA is already leaning over INGENUE. She kisses her. INGENUE starts back momentarily, blocked by the piano. DIVA persists, undoing the top button of INGENUE's blouse… But as the lights change she turns away, towards the audience.

DIVA: In an American desert – once Sacred Land – sits an Indian squaw, as old as she is wise.

If you pay her due reverence (and the necessary number of cigarettes), she will invite you to sit opposite her. And perhaps she will tell you the story of the Morning Star, who led the sun up into the sky, and the Evening Star, who drove the sun down to darkness.

She will tell how the myth of the Morning Star reached its ritual climax in four-year cycles… It seems the young warriors of the tribe were called upon to creep up to an enemy camp and capture a woman who must be young and must be beautiful. This they would do and they would take her back to their own territory, where she was treated with great kindness by the elderly and adulation by the young because – it was believed – she could carry good messages to the gods, herself – you understand – now enjoying a status half-goddess, half-woman.

Then, after many moons had passed and in the afternoon of an appointed day, the young beautiful woman was stripped naked and painted half red and half black to symbolise the Morning and Evening Stars. Then she was tied to a scaffold and the young warriors killed her with a shower of arrows. Her blood was believed to revive an ancient blessing from the gods and to ensure good fortune over the next four years.

The girl herself – the beautiful young woman – was, you see, no longer necessary, would with time and age have become an embarrassment. But like this her memory, her inspiration, her legend would live on.

In Berlin they had said to me, 'Happy the woman who has such great beauty.' I said to them, 'Unhappy the woman who needs such beauty'…

They said, 'Happy the woman whom men constantly remind of her beauty.' I said, 'Unhappy the woman who needs reminding. Unhappy those men who feel the need to remind…'

In the desert I searched for the old Indian woman. I wanted to say, 'Yes. The users and the used? This I know. The Morning Star, the Evening Star? Even this I can accept.'

…But also I would have asked: 'For those who have outgrown the Morning and not yet reached the Evening, who have become weary of the sun yet fearful of the dark, how best do we survive the long Afternoon?'

I did not find the old woman. Perhaps, after all, I did not need to…

I smoked my cigarettes alone.

Before she leaves the stage, DIVA pauses: the 'JANITOR' has appeared and seems to look at her. She walks off.

Lights come up again on the office sanctum where the 'JANITOR' is seen crouching down with difficulty as he begins to draw from beneath the chair a strangely battered suitcase.

SW: *(Off.)* Hello?… Hello?

A shaft of light as of a door just opened.

'JANITOR': What <u>is</u> this? Open House?

Guiltily, he pushes the case back under the chair with his foot. He turns as the SONGWRITER enters, burning up.

SW: There you are… Hey, Old Fellah, what d'you say? What d'you think?

SONGWRITER turns his backside towards the 'JANITOR'. He unbuckles the belt of his trousers as if ready to drop them. He leans forward, sticking out his rear.

'JANITOR': I think I've seen better…

SW: Why so shy all of a sudden? Stick it to me!

'JANITOR': At my time of life? To be offered such riches?

SONGWRITER buttons up, turns, still on fire.

SW: Then tell me what the fuck that 'meeting' was all about? That...<u>mutant</u> through there? Tell me that you and the Company don't wanna fuck me up the ass! Well?

'JANITOR': You're speaking to the wrong man, Ernie...

SONGWRITER advances towards 'JANITOR'.

SW: This 'mutant', this...bubble-brain – he thinks he can talk to me like yesterday I just got out the shtetl? I've never been so insulted in my life!

'JANITOR': *(Light.)* Well, it's early yet.

SW: ?

'JANITOR': Ernie, Ernie. Calm yourself... Okay –

SW: Why did God create the orgasm? So dickheads like him would know when to stop screwing!

'JANITOR': – I should have warned you.

SW: Was this how you guys treated <u>Buddie</u>?

'JANITOR': Hey, Ernie. Hear the one about the queer deaf mute?

SW: Can't say I did.

'JANITOR': Neither did he. You ain't queer and you ain't mute –

SW: Well thank you –

'JANITOR': But you're kinda <u>deaf</u>. I'm trying to tell you. <u>I had nothing to do with this</u>. Look around. *(Gestures to the space.)* Tomorrow all this goes into storage. And me along with it.

SW: What? Since when?

'JANITOR': Since yesterday afternoon.

SW: They've turned on you too? 'Cos they knew you were on our side? Hey, Old Fellah... *(Begins to move towards him in a conciliatory embrace.)*

'JANITOR': *(Smiles ruefully.)* I'm sorry to disappoint you, Ernie. No. They did not think I was 'on your side'. Why should they? Me the Company Man?

SW: Then –

'JANITOR': Not that I approve what they're doing...

SW: What <u>are</u> they doing?

'JANITOR': ...Matter of fact, may they all die slow and painful.

SW: Then what are we talking here? Corporation Politics, back East? –

'JANITOR': You could say that...

SW: Some boardroom putsch? A coup d'état?

'JANITOR': I managed to bat 400, Ernie. How many bat a thousand?... Listen. The guy's not asking the moon –

SW: I'm sorry?

'JANITOR': He's just asking a little 'co-operation'.

SW: This I'm hearing from <u>you</u>? '<u>Harry Konig</u>'?

Pause.

'JANITOR': Like I said: I oughta have warned you...

SW: *(Scarcely hearing.)* You're either with them or you're against them. This ain't the way to go. You most of all. You, Harry Konig, who had more balls than anyone I ever met... <u>Protest</u>, for Christ's sake. Or why not try The Response Evasive – tell 'em to go fuck 'emselves.

'JANITOR': This I tried.

SW: Then tell 'em... I don't know, tell 'em to hold off a year. Tell 'em you've got a heart condition, you're already two strokes down and just waiting for the bell. Tell 'em a year from now you won't even be here and <u>then</u> –

'JANITOR': This I tried also. Big mistake. They smelled blood...

SW: ?

'JANITOR': And it happens to be true.

SW: What?

Pause.

'JANITOR': Ernie. You're like a son to me. Always have been…

SW: Sure. 'Abraham and Isaac'.

'JANITOR': D'you recall the first time you came out West? You stood where you're standing now. Remember how you said you wanted to write songs for the people? The everyday people? People who sure as hell couldn't afford Broadway prices but they could at least afford two tickets on a Saturday night down the corner movie-house?

SW: You were great, Harry. You were the best…

'JANITOR': And I said –

SW: You said: 'Let no one, let nothing stand in your way. No scruple of conscience…'

'JANITOR': 'Show 'em, we Jews –'

SW: 'We don't go under.'

'JANITOR': 'Show 'em we Jews –'

SW: 'We <u>survive</u>'.

Pause.

SW: And now?

'JANITOR': Hey, if enough people tell you you're drunk, <u>lie down</u>.

SW: ?

'JANITOR': Have the last laugh, Ernie…

SW: 'He who laughs last didn't get the joke.'

'JANITOR': … Go with the flow. <u>Adapt</u>. They want a clean stable. Me, I'm 'Ancien Régime'.

SW: You buy that?

'JANITOR': I have a choice? Besides, they'll make it worth my while –

SW: Harry –

'JANITOR': I'm not a young man any more. Now I say, 'Of two temptations, I choose the one that gets me home soonest'. And – you would agree – thanks to the dough a comfortable home it is. The pool. The chauffeur. The private movie theater… I'm on my way out. But, Ernie, you still got thirty years. There's still gold in these-here hills. The gold that comes with fine music, the gold that buys a fire to warm you and a place in the hearts and minds, hell, if you want it, that buys you a new Bechstein, a high-gloss limo and a high-gloss floosie on each arm too… Listen to me. What's a few names after all? Throw 'em a bone. Throw 'em a big one – and slip away home again while they're still licking their lips.

Pause.

Well? You go back in there and make your peace? You drop the objections?

SW: Or just my pants? I start out as a lion…and I end up as a sacrificial lamb.

'JANITOR' shrugs, suddenly exhausted again.

'JANITOR': It's up to you. He's waiting, Ernie. Just two doors down.

SONGWRITER stands facing downstage, irresolute, thinking it through.

So? What d'you say?

Lights dim slowly on them in these positions.

Interval.

A light up on INGENUE, downstage.

INGENUE: So there we were, Mom and me – see, Mom was my 'chaperone', and we all had to have a 'chaperone' – there we were the two of us, bussed over to Austin real nice and put up in this swell hotel. 'Cept the Event itself, this was in an indoor stadium, and when we first got there they told us how it worked, what we had to do – they called this The Induction – so soon I learned there was as many as thirty of us all told but Mom said, 'No question! Talent? Personality? Poise? Did God really <u>want</u> me to be second-bested by Lois Greenberg?'

Well, that first day we had to rehearse like crazy until they held the Swimsuit part of the competition, and you walk out on your high heels along this ramp to a circle, praying you won't fall over, remembering like you got an imaginary string holding your head erect, remembering you got to <u>glide</u> and neither swing the arms too much or hold them too stiff neither 'cos that'd make things just as worse, and always afraid the swimsuit it's riding up at the back where you forgot to tape it but you don't dare reach back and pull it down with all them hundreds of eyes on you, not to mention the photographers, and you turn once ever so slowly so the judges <u>and</u> the crowd <u>and</u> the photographers they can get a good look at your ankles and your thighs and your ass. (Of course, Lois Greenberg said this was all 'degrading'. Naturally she would! I ask you: what's 'degrading' about your ass unless it looks like Lois Greenberg's?)

And so then after another day's rehearsal came the last and major Event – full evening-gown and four-button-gloves 'n' all – and all the flashing bulbs and all the people out there, this time in their tuxedos, and there was this big banquet <u>before</u> the main show – can you believe it? I mean, I couldn't eat a thing if they was paying me, which I guess in a way they was! – and then an introduction by the Mayor and – hey! that's when I first heard Mr Case's song? 'Blue Heart Afternoon?' – full orchestra and all! they said it was

49

the Song Of The Year!… Before I knew it, we were down to ten and then five, would you believe, and – some reason I don't understand, Lois Greenberg, she was still in there, hair down to her shoulders like some dime-store Veronica Lake and so padded out front it made you feel you was about to be run over – and then each of us was asked to speak for one minute no more no less to the gentleman holding a microphone, they called him The Master Of Ceremonies, on 'How Would You Make The World A Better Place?'

Lois Greenberg was ahead of me and, of course, <u>she</u> said with that stuck-up goodie-goodie voice of hers she's had since Junior High, 'I think we should just learn to love each other a little more, all creeds, religions and races…' I mean – Yuh! Pass me the sick bag, right? So when it came to <u>my</u> turn 'Tell us, Jennifer: How Would <u>You</u> Make The World A Better Place?' I was about to say, 'Well, you could start by pushing Lois Greenberg off a cliff,' but, see, I was smart, I told them good and straight: 'I don't know too much about them other creeds, religions and races. All I know as a true American is that now more than ever we gotta defend ourselves against them out there who want to destroy this the best Country in the World, with this the best Way of Life in the World…'

… And, well, tra-la-la, that's how I came to win 'Miss Texas 1950'. 'Cos win it I truly did. And, well, – there you have the whole story of me thinking, Jennifer my girl, from here on out it's only a short step to Movie-Stardom, and then me coming out here to Hollywood and…as for Lois Greenberg – <u>Who</u>??

Lights up on INGENUE and SONGWRITER in SONGWRITER's apartment.

SW: *(Outraged.)* You did <u>what</u>?

INGENUE: You heard.

SW: You mean…'all the way'?

INGENUE: Correct!

SW: But I was only gone a couple of hours! I'm not just outraged, I'm…<u>disappointed</u>! I didn't mean you to have sex with her, did I?

INGENUE: What <u>did</u> you mean, Mr Case?

SW: At the very least you might have <u>waited</u>.

INGENUE: So you could join in, maybe?

SW: I mean, till she and I had finished our business. Settled our deal.

INGENUE: Seems to me like maybe I was <u>part</u> of the deal.

SW: Come now…

A morose silence between them. Then:

SW: Good, was it?

Despite herself, INGENUE laughs at the candour of the question.

INGENUE: Kind of exciting. I guess.

SW: You 'guess'?

INGENUE: I never tried it before. Not with another woman, I mean. I don't know what came over me.

SW: 'New Territory', right?

INGENUE: That's what <u>she</u> said.

SW: *(Imitating DIVA's accent.)* 'It is only occasionally "geographical".'

INGENUE: I'm sorry?

Another pause.

SW: *(Small-Boy charm.)* Forgive me?

She moves into his open arms.

So tell me. How was <u>your</u> meeting with Harry Konig?

She breaks away from his embrace, tidies up her mussed hair etc.

INGENUE: I ought to be getting back... Mr Konig, I don't believe he has time for people like me.

Promise me something, Ernie. Promise you won't tell Mr Konig – or anyone else – I'm just another no-hope actress working as a waitress, another loser who thinks if she sleeps around enough... Well, you know the rest.

SW: Now would I say a thing like that?

INGENUE: You know... When I came out here I wasn't asking too much, I thought. *(Smiles wanly.)* Just to be a star!... And if I couldn't be a star, at least I might get to be a stand-in. And if I couldn't be a stand-in, well, at least I'd see what else they was offering. Now I'm not so sure. Now...

She holds it a sad moment, thoughtful.

Finally, consolingly:

SW: Hey. You're my Texas Rose.

INGENUE: Sure. 'Second-hand Rose'. *(A beat.)* I'm sorry, Mr Case.

SW: What for?

INGENUE: 'Cos – in spite of everything – you're a nice man? *(Turning to go.)* Hey – I gotta get back to my shift.

She starts to leave downstage.

SW: Jennifer?

She looks back.

Look me up, okay?

INGENUE: *(Suddenly bright again.)* Sure thing!

She goes. SONGWRITER is left, lost in thought, to wander around the apartment, hands in pockets. He spots her make-up case still on the ground under the piano and pokes it with his foot, amused/sad that it's been forgotten once more. He wanders over to the piano, plays a few bluesy chords, stops. He goes over to the radio, tunes it briefly to a station:

'was "Blue Heart Afternoon" sung by Frank Sinatra.'

For a moment, SONGWRITER beams, looking at the radio proudly. The moment is, however, short-lived...

'(Jingle/Music.) This is the three p.m. news from WLA serving the Greater Los Angeles area... At a press conference in Washington DC this morning, Senator McCarthy reiterated his commitment to what he described as the "moral crusade" of the House Un-American Activities Committee against quote "Communist infiltration of the entertainment industry and in particular of –" '

Lights come down, the radio broadcast just carrying over into the beginning of the next scene.

The office sanctum – now more desolate than ever.

The 'JANITOR' stands without jacket, tie or collar, but his shirt-sleeves still clipped by expensive arm-garters and cufflinks. He seems to be engaged in sorting through a pile of clothes and old mementoes including photographs. Each item is considered momentarily before being placed (or replaced?) in the small battered suitcase seen previously and now open at his feet.

'JANITOR': My wife thinks I've gone mad, Mama. Says if I don't come home straight away, she 'won't be responsible'! *(Laughs.)* Responsible for <u>what</u>?, I ask. And anyway – where's 'home'? The place where you hang your head? Or the place where, when you have to go there, they have to take you in?

Always I said, 'Leave with a smile. You might wanna come back.' Well, I wanna come back, Mama. Is that so impossible? When all day long my clock's been running backwards?

Well, what d'you say? Soon – soon – I'll be that little boy again you couldn't bear to see go.

He continues to place some things in the case, discarding others.

Papa – <u>he</u> could bear to see me go. But that's another story…

Continuing to scrutinise, place or discard the different objects…

Do you see me now, Mama? I'm running so quick that, as I pass, whole cities un-build themselves, proud new office-blocks tumble back into the slums they were before… Now I un-learn my American, now I trade in my fedora for a good Berlin homburg. Well – 'if the glove fits…'

He holds a homburg out in front of him, punches it into shape and tilts it jauntily on his head.

…and – how d'you like that? – this pain, even this pain across my chest and all down my side I had since this morning, it's almost gone! I'm almost whole again. I'm crossing at a lick Rosenthaler Platz, a bowl of fleishik kept warm in my handkerchief, and already in the air the first promise of snow. Spring turning winter and winter fall…

He takes off his cufflinks and arm-garters and deposits them. He picks up a jacket – old, frayed – and puts it on, clearly gratified by its shabbiness. The transformation is complete: he has become, again, an émigré.

And here I am at last, Mama, standing in front of the door – your door – closed but with a light underneath which tells me you are not asleep. If only I could open it…but already I've gotten too small, too weak. 'Just one more push'. I hear you, Mama. Yes, just one more push and instead of a room there will be a garden lined with linden and plane trees and a table covered in starched white linen, laid for afternoon chocolate. And you are there with Grandma and Grandpa, all of you seated, all of you smiling. And you have been waiting oh so patiently, telling me take my time, what's the rush? And now, Mama, already the light behind you is brighter, the light getting brighter all the time and still you are smiling: 'Harry, come now. Come to my arms. You know you can.'

He leans down, snaps the case shut and picking it up turns to where a light source through an opening door is getting stronger.

…And I can. Because now, at last, everything is possible.

Suitcase in hand, he begins to walk towards the light. But the door now widens till the light from behind it blazes as bright and fierce as death itself, freezing him in his tracks.

Blackout.

Lights up slowly. The SONGWRITER's apartment.

Long and low shafts of sunlight tell us we are now at the end of the afternoon or in early evening.

The telephone is ringing insistently.

Eventually, SONGWRITER appears. He is fixing with some difficulty his cufflinks (now he wears dinner-suit trousers and a dress shirt open at the collar with as yet no tie) while also attempting to cradle a cup of coffee. He answers the phone.

SW: Yes?… He <u>what</u>? When?… But I just… How d'you hear? –

DIVA appears.

Listen. Thanks. I'll get back to you…

He hangs up.

DIVA comes in: she is stunning in evening gown, heels and discreet jewels.

SW: What a surprise! My, did you put that frock on just for little ol' me?

DIVA: There's a benefit for Buddie, remember?

SW: No kidding. If this is how you look for a wake, what do you wear on a Saturday night?

DIVA: And you? Ain't that the beginnings of a dress suit?

SW: Buddie was a good man.

DIVA: Right.

SW: *(Ushering her in.)* To what do I owe this pleasure? Tonight you want me as your escort? Gigolo? Fancy man?

DIVA: I leave here, I've no sooner got home –

SW: How about a drink?

DIVA: I have no sooner told my agent that the movie, <u>your</u> movie, forgive me, but I'm less than enthralled –

SW: How about I make that <u>two</u> drinks?

DIVA: I've no sooner told my agent than, what d'you know, a call comes through from the studio –

SW: Suggesting you do my movie?

DIVA: Suggesting I come in next week and 'explain myself', there's a gentleman who wants to ask me a few 'informal' questions!

You telling me this is pure coincidence, Mister? One moment I'm here, the next I get an 'informal' summons from Washington?

SONGWRITER calmly prepares her a drink.

SW: Believe it or not, I'm pleased to see you. Really I am.

DIVA: Excuse me?

SW: I get back from the studio, have me a snooze and I dream about you… You're up in a painting in Europe somewhere. A courtesan. 'Quattrocento.'

He hands her her drink.

DIVA: What's this to me, Big Boy?

SW: Some danger. Some dark disorder just barely hinted in the depths of her…your…sea-green eyes. In my dream you were great. You'd just quit talking.

DIVA: And what had I 'just quit' saying?

SW: You'd said –
'Hey Daddy –
Let me take you

Down…

Down…

Down…'

DIVA: You've been drinking too much coffee.

SW: Can <u>anyone</u> buy you, Diva? What <u>is</u> your price?

DIVA: Pardon me?

SW: Because, waking up, I say to myself, 'This is Diva', right?
The most famous face in Europe and America combined.
Let's turn that one around. Let's ask what she's doing
coming over here talking – to a mere songwriter, no less
– about some movie she don't like and she don't need to
make? Could it be she's 'checking me out'? Could it be <u>she</u>
has some other agenda? Could it be that the 'gentleman
from Washington' she now casually mentions is not a New
Enemy but an Old Friend?

DIVA: I think you just said goodbye to your leading lady…

SW: Let's just spool back, shall we? When d'you get here? '34?
'35?

DIVA: You want my memoirs? '34.

SW: Right! Back home – '32 – you're already peaking…

DIVA: Thank you.

SW: '33, you're worried you've lost it…

DIVA: One of us must be drowning. My whole life is flashing
before your eyes.

SW: Then in '34 – bingo – you're outa there. '35, '36, you're
here home and dry. A bigger star than ever.

DIVA: I'm still waiting for the other shoe to drop…

SW: You heard about those guys, those Nazis, who came here
from Europe and made the A–bomb?

DIVA: I heard.

SW: They weren't too fussy about changing sides either.

DIVA: Ah, I get it! I'm secretly a rocket-scientist! Einstein in drag!

SW: There's a mystery about you, Diva.

DIVA: As you say – it made me a star.

SW: It made you <u>untrustworthy</u>… Well?

DIVA: Yes, I have my own 'agenda'. Who doesn't? –

SW: Those war years, when you were struggling to prove your new 'loyalty' to all things American? –

DIVA: Yes, I came to 'check you out' –

SW: You made friends in high places. You made promises. And now here we are: payback time.

Is this how you move on – into your 'new territory'? This movie of mine – was it ever more than just a pretext for you to come around and sniff me out?

DIVA: Not entirely.

SW: ?

DIVA: You saw my last movie…

SW: So what? You're protected by the studio. Always have been.

DIVA: Says who?

SW: You have a contract.

DIVA: It's up for renewal.

SW: Then…I don't get it!

DIVA merely returns his look. SONGWRITER throws his hands in the air.

DIVA: You met with Harry Konig? How is he?

SW: 'Harry Konig'? Fuck Harry Konig!

DIVA: How was the meeting?

SW: It was like Harry himself. Kinda brutal. Kinda short on civility.

DIVA: ?

SW: But sometimes God is quick to avenge! Harry, I just heard, has suddenly been taken sick…though rumors of a heart attack seem implausible if only because most medics in the Greater Los Angeles area would confess ignorance as to where – if <u>anywhere</u> – the heart of Harry Konig is yet to be located.

DIVA nods gravely, momentarily covering her face with her hands. Oblivious, SONGWRITER continues:

It's feeding time for the piranhas, lady. The House Un-American Activities Committee has narrowed its focus, has even started getting interested in the likes of little ol' me, has decided it won't leave the studios to clean their own stable; they'll come in and do it themselves.

They're talking the end of the studio, the end of the industry as we know it, and World War Three with the Soviets a couple of years down the line.

DIVA: And in reality?

SW: In reality a few movies put on hold, half a dozen actors told to find themselves a lawyer while they, er, take the mountain air. Also in there somewhere – bottom of the food chain, so to speak – the occasional writer or musician like yours truly – advised that back East is where one always belonged, why not go back there, the company might prove more congenial.

Hey – you okay?

DIVA: So if Harry's been taken sick who <u>did</u> you see?

SW: Oh I saw Harry. Matter of fact, Harry was packing his bags…

DIVA: ?

SW: *(Sardonic.)* Harry having to pack his own bags for once? Hey, maybe we should blame his heart attack on a chronic shortage of servants? *(Registering her impatience, he finally pulls out of his back pocket a business card.)* I was duly ushered into the presence of one 'Thomas Rankin', from Washington DC, a man in a grey suit with a very, very quiet manner, at present employed by the House Un-American Activities Committee of said Washington DC and currently investigating 'Communist affiliation and loyalty' among members of the Screenwriters' Guild and the Composers' And Musicians' Union. No doubt the same gentleman you'll be meeting next week.

He has put away the card.

He wanted names.

His elbows propped on his knees, he slowly raises his hands to cradle his head. A moment.

DIVA: Ernie?

SW: *(Rallying somewhat.)* Hey. That's a first! That's the first time you've called me 'Ernie' –

DIVA: You and this…'Rankin'. Did you give him the names? Don't tell me what I think I'm going to hear, all right? I'd rather leave now.

SW: Then leave you should 'cos this afternoon I disgraced myself, my father and his father before him.

'Ernie,' my grandfather'd say. 'Do what you gotta do. Go out there and sell yourself!'

Well, this afternoon I sat there in Harry Konig's office, on Harry Konig's legendary couch – a couch which in its time has seen so much Innocence meet so much Experience… And what did I do? <u>What did I do</u>? There in front of my brain so I couldn't escape them I had the names, all the names, of my charming former pinko friends – names, I was thinking, they surely know in Washington anyway, so what the hell – and there too was that picture of my grandfather saying, 'Ernie! Ernie! Success at any price!'

DIVA: And?

SW: And still I couldn't do it!

DIVA: ?

SW: *(Furious with himself.)* I could not give those names.

He beats the side of his head with his palm.

Buddie and me. You know, we went through school together. Shared that flea-infested apartment in the Village, a lot of girls and a thousand plates of pasta while we waited for the first break – his first play, my first song.

Why did Buddie kill himself? Not 'cos he'd lost his job. Buddie could have been happy in a log cabin up in Canada, banging out novels on that old Remington of his. Not even – so I hear – 'cos he'd recently made a fool of himself leaving his wife of twenty years for some piece of ass scarcely out of diapers! No. Buddie killed himself 'cos he was afraid he was about to lose his light. His faith. In Stalin. In the Revolution.

Generous, big-hearted Buddie! Who was at one and the same time the smartest and the most naïve man I ever knew. Who, for all his brilliance, believed that everything would be well if we could just love each other a little more, if – don't ask me why – we took a few lessons from Karl Marx and Leon Trotsky, if the second half of the century could live up to our expectations for the first, if America's afternoon could be as fine, as idealistic and as high-minded as its morning.

He is lost in thought a moment. Finally:

Hear that? It's the sound of my grandfather turning in his grave saying 'Ernie, Ernie – your career, your future – all this you throw away for the sake of a few worthless goyem who are soft on Russia?!'

And my answer: 'Yes, Gramps. After all these years, after so much love and devotion, so much education and expense, I, your own grandson, little Ernie Kasitski, have turned out to be that worst and most unfortunate of all Americans: a Jew with the conscience of a Puritan!'

He slumps down again, head in hands, brooding.

Mr Rankin from Washington is not pleased. Mr Rankin from Washington has said he will be filing his report in due course and no doubt his superiors will be anxious to discuss my quote 'uncooperative attitude' with my employers – my, er, <u>new</u> employers…

DIVA: What about Harry?

SW: Diva?

DIVA: How is Harry?

SW: Have you been listening to a single word? Fuck 'Harry Konig', I say! Why should <u>you</u> care?

DIVA: *(Shrugs.)* Because…once upon a time there was a very sweet man who took me to the theater in Berlin, bought me chocolates and said 'Liebchen, let me help you find the light and I can make you a star… And for this I will ask only one thing: you never let my wife or anyone else know that you and I are anything more than friends.' And that man was true to his word. He took this clumsy little German girl out of the afternoon salons, the rooms of frozen corruption and their men already in evening dress, with faces shaved silvery-smooth and every gesture its price. He took her out of the smokey, citied fear of death and the smell of something yet to come even worse than death, and brought her here to Hollywood. And made her a star.

SW: But this was Fritzi, right? Your first husband? Half the world knows that story…

DIVA: Only because Fritzi would have them believe it so while he pursued his little boys. Only because for everyone concerned it was the perfect cover.

Pause.

SW: *(Incredulous.)* Konig?

DIVA: That man of whom no one will say a good word. That man who hid his heart behind the shield of profanity and the sword of vulgarity the better to keep at bay the bureaucrats, the accountants and the corporate lawyers all of whom will take over his studio when he is gone. What am I saying? Who now <u>already</u>, it seems, are taking it over even <u>before</u> he is gone... That man, you say, stroked out in the Hollywood Hills who I cannot visit or even send flowers to for fear of alerting his wife – his guardian and jailer.

Pause.

SW: Get the fuck out of here.

DIVA: Excuse me?

SW: No sale, lady. Get the fuck out of here!

DIVA: What?

SW: You heard. Before I make you.

DIVA: ?

SW: Now it all makes sense. Now, at last, it all comes clear... You're losing your 'protector', right? Message comes through to your agent: Harry's about to be sacked; in twenty-four hours he won't be around any more. Your agent calls you. Once. Twice. Three times. 'Get your ass back here. Before word spreads, get back here and do what needs to be done. Check out Buddie's old gang.' –

DIVA: Hey –

SW: 'Whisper their names to the studio before the studio moves on. Before they move on without <u>you</u>!'

DIVA: Listen –

SW: Get out. Or else.

He moves threateningly towards her.

DIVA: Hey. If you touch me, I'll call a cop.

SW: If I touch you, you'll call an ambulance. Just 'cos you're a Blonde that don't make me a Gentleman.

DIVA: I believe you… But 'Payback time'? 'Promises'? Don't flatter yourself. You're not so important.

Incandescent, SONGWRITER is beginning to crowd her.

Yes I came here. Yes I was prepared to climb in my automobile, soiled from the desert and drag myself over here. Why? Because it seemed appropriate, on this day of all days when I'd be commemorating Buddie with some of his best friends, to see if this same Ernie Case, so anxious for me to give an aura of respectability to his self-justifying, self-promoting half-ass movie project –

SW: Hey!

DIVA: – To see if this same Ernie Case hadn't also helped Buddie to his grave by whispering what he knew about him to Washington. And, if this should indeed prove the case, I would pass it on, pass the word – not to Washington, no, to what you might call another little Conspiracy altogether: the Friends of Buddie, myself included, protecting our own.

Of course, little did I realize: I needn't have bothered. I mean, who's more desperate here? This supposedly famous songwriter…or me? And who's now persecuting who all of a sudden? Who's the victim and who the aggressor?… And you dare call me a 'Nazi'?!

SW: THAT TEARS IT!

He plunges forward, fist raised. DIVA steps back a pace, holds up a warning finger for him to keep his distance. He ignores it. She slaps him. He slaps her back. She punches him in the eye. He goes down.

SW: Jesus! –

Howling, he staggers up and back. Absurdly, he lurches to the sofa and crashes down, doubled up in pain.

Aghast, DIVA gulps, hesitates a moment and dashes over to the ice bucket as SONGWRITER writhes in agony on the sofa…To which DIVA returns, nursing ice cubes in a napkin. She sits quickly on the end of the sofa by his head.

DIVA: Oh for God's sake. Lie down, close your eyes, and shut up…

SW: That was meant to be my line.

He yelps with pain again. She applies the handkerchief and ice cubes.

DIVA: Perhaps you will remember this next time you seek to visit violence upon women.

SW: Was that really necessary? I was only going to shake you a little… And then maybe throttle you… And then maybe stamp on your grave. And for this – *(She's put his head in her lap, ministering further to his eye.)* Ouch! For this you take out an eye? This I call The Response Disproportionate. Ouch!

DIVA: Just keep quiet, will you? I can't look at this if you insist on talking.

He groans…but the pain is subsiding. Still crouched over him with the ice and handkerchief:

Funny. You have quite nice eyes…

SW: I used to! And now I only have one of 'em! *(Groans again.)* How am I expected to write my music when I'm blind in one eye?

DIVA: *(Chuckles.)* Or stamp on my grave when you can't even stand up straight?

SW: You're enjoying this, aren't you?

He continues groaning. She finishes attending to his eye.

DIVA: You'll live.

She throws down the wet napkin and ice. She lifts a hand to her head.

DIVA: Terrible…

SW: My eye?

DIVA: My hair. It's all mussed up.

SW: Hey. Can we establish some priorities here?

Pause.

DIVA: 'Priorities'? '<u>Priorities</u>'? *(Beat.)* Mr Case. Ernie. When you look at me you're looking at a woman whose sun is past its zenith and who now, it seems, has lost her protector. Who somewhere in the world has the remains of a family – a grown daughter, cousins who are attempting to live in Europe Year Five…

You are looking at a woman who is more needy than she wants anyone, including herself, ever to realize. And whose mind, despite itself, is now on penultimate things… Thank you but I believe I am aware of my 'priorities'.

SW: Then if <u>you</u> didn't tell 'em, how come Rankin almost <u>gave</u> me those names he wanted so much to hear? How come he seemed to know my every movement, who my friends were, who I played tennis with, who I'd even been sleeping with and…

He stops in mid-sentence. He and she look at each other. The penny drops just as INGENUE enters.

Shocked, SONGWRITER sits up abruptly – only to register a terrible pain in his eye. With a silent groan of agony he slumps back on the sofa..

INGENUE: Hi! I just came back to pick up my make-up box.

She sees DIVA, looks back at SONGWRITER, registers with a raised eyebrow his casualty status and the debris on the floor.

Is this a bad moment?

Nodding to the SONGWRITER's bruised temple:

… You finally collided with your Just Desserts?

SONGWRITER scowls…

INGENUE is now transformed, wearing a beret, also a stylized trench-coat which she unbuttons to reveal – 'accidentally' – a trouser suit of the kind one would expect DIVA to wear. Her former hesitancy is giving way to a more confrontational mode: suddenly she looks like a star in the making.

INGENUE: *(She looks up at the ceiling.)* Tell me. Have you ever thought of changing the lighting in here? All of a sudden it makes you look <u>old</u>.

DIVA: So, liebchen, at last you got yourself a script.

INGENUE: I've got nothing against you, Mr Case –

SW: *(Sharp. W.C.Fields:)* 'Well, <u>there</u>'s a relief!'

INGENUE: Besides. You should really be thanking me. Didn't I make another special trip to the studio this afternoon just to reassure them you were way too insignificant to be bothering with? You and the lady both, I'm guessing. *(Back to SONGWRITER.)* I figured you wouldn't get into any <u>real</u> trouble, with the Committee 'n' all. Oh no. Not if you were sensible and grown-up about it. Who knows? – maybe one day we'll work on a movie together. Mr Rankin has been very grateful. Says he'll make sure I get on the studio payroll. He says they really need the kind of girl who's proved herself a True American. He says he'll make me a star.

SW: Snitching for Washington ain't a full-time activity?

INGENUE: I don't call it 'snitching'. Mr Rankin don't call it 'snitching' either. Only a certain kind of mentality would call it that – the kind of mentality which gets investigated in the first place… Besides, 's not only you they've been investigating – oh no. There's half a dozen. A lot more important than <u>you</u>.

SW: Oh my God. Buddie!… 'The piece of ass scarcely out of diapers'! –

DIVA: And you, er, 'researched' them too, did you?

INGENUE: Everything I've done, well – I've done it on purpose. I've done it for the good of my country. Not for fame. Not for money. And not for other more… 'degrading' reasons neither. Excuse me…

In a single movement she scoops up her make-up case and heads for the door – only to turn back at the last moment.

When you get to a certain age – *(She looks at them bashfully then defiantly.)* – then maybe it's time to start behaving with just a little more 'dignity'?

Know what I mean?

She turns on her heel and is gone.

A moment. DIVA and SONGWRITER are stunned. He stands as if (too late) about to protest…

Finally he turns away, beginning to laugh – this in turn mutating into a stifled sob…

DIVA: Ernie? Ernie?

Some moments – his hands still over his face.

A long pause while he gathers himself.

Finally he limps to the piano where, preoccupied, he starts to play some soft consolatory chords.

Think it's any better for me? You don't depend on your looks – <u>thank God</u> you don't depend on your looks. Me, it's my bread and butter. Once <u>they</u> go…

SW: *(Flat; factual.)* Once <u>they</u> go, you do cabaret. I foresee a glittering future, the whole world over. Trust me.

He continues playing, locked in his thoughts.

DIVA: I put in a call to Buddie's wife this afternoon, Ernie.

He continues playing.

She told me how you and Buddie went through school together, how – after – you roomed together in New York City. How that long, cold winter before Buddie got his first break, when he fell sick you fed him every second hour on soup and noodles, nursed him all day every day and – so she says – virtually kept him alive till you damn near got sick yourself with the cold and the hunger and the exhaustion of it.

He continues, expressionless.

So it was true after all. Hard times in the Village. Penury and pasta.

SW: *(Shrugs.)* Would I lie to you?

DIVA: She also told me how <u>before</u> school, <u>before</u> New York City, you grew up practically next door to him. In Buffalo. In the same, rich-man's suburb of Buffalo. So she tells me.

Pause. SONGWRITER momentarily stops playing. Still preoccupied with his own thoughts, he seems unfazed by her last remark as he stares blankly at the keyboard in front of him.

DIVA: Ernie?

SW: Mm?

SW: Ernie. If you're looking for a poor childhood full of overcrowded tenements, fire escapes and kids dying of meningitis, you don't go to a rich suburb of Buffalo.

SW: *(Bogart.)* 'Then I guess I was misinformed.'

He shrugs and starts playing again. Now he plays the same Schubert-into-the blues motif we heard in the first part. Some moments until, still playing, he looks up, smiling wearily.

SW: Diva – this is 'America', right? You come out of the darkness to find the light. You start Polish or German; you end up on Broadway or in Hollywood. You're born rich but you learn to play the blues 'cos it's the blues the people came to hear… Ain't that what we do, you and I? We change the words to fit the tune? You telling me that stops there from being some kinda truth underneath it all? A truth that can move people to tears or laughter by whatever route we came to it?

He continues to strike soft chords thoughtfully.

DIVA: So now? Fade to black? Goodnight and good luck?

SW: I told you: I go back East and you become 'a legend'.

DIVA: That simple?

SW: That simple.

She moves to the piano, sits beside him as he continues to play chords softly.

DIVA: I guess I never told you why I went to the desert.

SW: To get away from a man?

DIVA: Not even.

SW: A woman?

DIVA: A boy. A mere boy. Normally I just purse my lips and tell them to come back ten years ago. Not this time. Not this one.

He told me he worshipped me. He told me he'd seen each of my movies ten, a dozen times.

SW: You believed him?

DIVA: He could quote me back my lines better than I could. Besides – he was very, very beautiful.

SW: You got him in the sack?

DIVA: I did. Except…

SW: [Yes]?

DIVA: He didn't even get a hard-on. Turned out it wasn't sex he wanted. It was so he could go home and brag about me to his boyfriend. Is this the best we can look forward to, you and me? Is this the 'New Territory'?

SW: *(Still playing notes.)* Want to try again? This time with a grown-up?

She laughs quietly as, momentarily, he stops playing. She raises a hand, gently stroking his bruised eye.

DIVA: Ernie, Ernie, Ernie. What shall we do with you?

SW: … And then, when we're done, we go and pay our respects to the memory of our good friend Buddie.

DIVA: On one condition.

SW: That I don't get a hard-on?

DIVA: That you play me that song of yours. 'Purple Afternoon'?

SW: '<u>Blue Heart</u> Afternoon'. You still ain't heard it?

DIVA: 'S all the rage, they say.

SW: You serious?

She places one hand on his shoulder, affectionately.

SW: You <u>are</u> serious.

Well, okay –

He takes a deep breath, lifts his hands to play – and blackout.

End of Play.

OTHER NIGEL GEARING TITLES

Dickens in America
9781840020663

Janis in the Chelsea
Elgar's Tenth Muse
Meeting Mr Wilde
9781840021615

WWW.OBERONBOOKS.COM

 Follow us on www.twitter.com/@oberonbooks
& www.facebook.com/oberonbook